PLANNING
YOUR WEDDING

PLANNING
YOUR WEDDING

Helen Fisher

CONSUMERS' ASSOCIATION

Which? Books are commissioned and researched by
Consumers' Association and published by
Which? Ltd,
2 Marylebone Road, London NW1 4DF
Email address: books@which.net

Distributed by The Penguin Group:
Penguin Books Ltd, 27 Wrights Lane, London W8 5TZ

First edition June 1998
Copyright © 1998 Which? Ltd

British Library Cataloguing in Publication Data
A catalogue record for this book is available from the British
Library

ISBN 0 85202 721 4

No part of this publication may be reproduced or transmitted in
any form or by any means, electronically or mechanically, including
photocopying, recording or any information storage or
retrieval system, without prior permission in writing from the
publishers. The publication is not included under licences issued
by the Copyright Agency.

For a full list of Which? books, please write to Which? Books,
Castlemead, Gascoyne Way, Hertford X, SG14 1LH
or access our website at http://www.which.net

Cartoons and cover illustration by David Pattison,
Cartoon Partnership
Typeset by Saxon Graphics Ltd, Derby
Printed and bound in Great Britain by St Edmundsbury Press,
Bury St Edmunds

Contents

	Introduction	7
1	Engagement	8
2	Timetable	15
3	Principal players	22
4	Wedding stationery	26
5	Dress and accessories	35
6	Photographs and videos	40
7	Flowers	44
8	Transport	48
9	Wedding cake	52
10	Music	54
11	Gifts	56
12	Reception	59
13	Ceremony	71

14	Insurance	76
	Appendix Wedding Law	80
	Addresses	92
	Index	93

Introduction

Organising a wedding involves all the planning of a military operation, whether it is in the village church, a synagogue, a register office or in a Gothic Scottish castle. As soon as you are engaged, the wedding machine will crank into gear and it is vital that you keep track of all the arrangements – and the costs.

Although it is estimated that the average cost of a wedding (including the honeymoon) in the UK is £10,000 you can get married in a register office for as little as £51 if bride and groom live in the same district as each other. It is very easy to overshoot your budget. Decide on it early on and stick to it.

This book will help you plan your wedding from start to finish. It includes price guidelines and questions to ask suppliers to ensure you get what you want, so that when the day itself dawns you will both be able to relax and enjoy one of the most memorable events in your life together.

And while no one wants to dwell too heavily on what might go wrong, there are some sensible suggestions you can follow to prevent slip-ups – as well as some warnings about *over*-insuring against them.

ENGAGEMENT

1

Once you have told both sets of parents that you are getting married, you need to let the rest of your family and friends know. It is traditional for the bride's mother to inform the bride's relations and close family friends, while the groom tells his own family and friends. However, nowadays many brides do this themselves. If you have close-knit families it is courteous to tell them all personally.

If you want to place a public announcement in the local or national press, now is the time to do so. Traditionally, the bride's parents announce the engagement of their daughter, but you may decide on the wording if you wish. If you are getting married for the second time you may prefer to organise the announcement yourselves.

A telephone call or letter to the 'Births, Marriages and Deaths' column of the newspaper giving the desired message and date you would like it to appear is all that is required, although you may prefer to put it in writing. Before deciding on the final wording, check how much it will cost: a lengthy announcement can be expensive.

The engagement period

After the initial excitement has died down, take the time to decide what kind of wedding you can really afford. Discuss the time, place and type of event you want and establish these as a framework for your plans. When you have decided on the type of wedding, you will need to think about music, flowers, honeymoon destinations, presents and so on.

Deciding on every last detail – from napkins to nuptials – requires ingenuity and, above all, tact. Whatever the scale of the wedding, sharing the workload is often the only way to pull the event together. So draw on all the support you can. Relations on both sides, as well as friends, may well wish to be involved and be eager to help.

Rings

Although the majority of engaged women wear an engagement ring, it is not compulsory to do so.

If you do decide to wear one you may have a number of options to choose from:

- a family heirloom
- one from an antique shop
- a new one from a jeweller
- one designed specially for you.

Antique rings can be better value for money, but should be checked by a professional jeweller. The stones in old rings are sometimes not as secure in their setting. Also, make sure you have the ring valued for insurance purposes. When buying a new ring, you will be given a certificate by the jeweller stating its value. You should be able to insure it on your house contents policy.

Rings vary tremendously in value. Much of the value is in the quality (carat) of the stone(s). Traditionally, the groom spends about one month's salary on the engagement ring, but do not regard this as a requirement — spend only what you can afford.

When you are looking at engagement rings in a shop try them on with a wedding ring. Consider how the two look together. Rings with an unusual design may not fit snugly next to a wedding ring so ask the jeweller whether a wedding ring can be made to fit next to it. Some engagement and wedding rings come as a set.

Whether or not you have to have a wedding ring depends on the type of service you are having. In the Church of England ceremony the bride must have a ring for the service to go ahead; in the Roman Catholic Church the giving or exchanging of rings is a standard part of the ceremony; in Scotland and in civil weddings in register offices it is not compulsory to have a wedding ring but it would be unusual for the service to take place without some token being exchanged. Rings are not a formal part of a Quaker wedding ceremony, although some couples do choose to exchange them. The bride must have a ring for the Jewish wedding ceremony.

Traditionally, wedding and engagement rings are worn on the fourth finger of the left hand. The band is usually made of gold, but platinum and silver are also popular. It is advisable to buy a wedding ring made of the same metal as the engagement ring so that they match. In addition, platinum is harder than 22-carat gold, for example, and over time (as they are worn next to each other) will wear the softer metal down.

Gold has to be mixed with other metals to give it strength and because of this it is classified according to the quantity of gold in the ring: the more gold present, the higher the carat. The purest is 22-carat, while 18-carat is less expensive and stronger. Nine-carat gold is cheaper and stronger again.

Gold varies in colour – from white through shades of yellow to a rosy red gold. A strong yellow shade is fashionable, but you might like to consider how it suits any precious stone in your engagement ring.

Platinum is a pure metal and naturally durable, so it will take many years of hard treatment. This quality and strength makes it a popular choice for men's wedding rings.

Silver is less expensive but be aware that it is not as long-lasting as gold or platinum. It tarnishes and eventually disintegrates on combining with oxygen in the atmosphere. Although this will not happen during a life time, over many years it will thin and show signs of knocks and scratches.

Wearing your wedding ring before the ceremony is considered unlucky.

PAYING FOR AND ORGANISING THE WEDDING

Traditionally, the bride's parents pay for most of the wedding, and the groom covers the rest.

The bride's parents pay for:

- the engagement announcement (in the press)
- the bride's dress
- the attendants' clothing
- flowers for the wedding and reception venues
- the photographs
- the wedding video

- the transport
- the reception
- invitations, order-of-service cards and place setting cards.

The groom pays for:

- the fees for the church, chapel or synagogue, including the heating if it is in winter, the bells, the organist, the fee if one is required for having the ceremony videoed
- the groom's and best man's clothing (if the best man has to hire a suit)
- the bride's and bridesmaids' bouquets, the buttonholes and the mothers' corsages
- the car to the wedding venue for the groom and best man
- the car to the honeymoon departure point
- engagement and wedding rings
- presents for the best man and the attendants
- the honeymoon.

However, nowadays the groom's parents usually share the cost of the wedding, and some couples (especially if they are older and are reasonably well off, or getting married for the second time) may also pay for part of it. Discuss, with both sets of parents, who can afford to pay for what and split the cost fairly.

Wedding organisers

Most couples organise the wedding themselves, with the help of either or both sets of parents. However, if you do not have the time you could consider getting a wedding organiser to do it all for you. Such companies advise on and organise anything from one or two aspects of the wedding to the whole thing. Most of them like to spend some time talking to the couple to find out what sort of people they are and what type of wedding they want. They will then liaise closely throughout the preparations. Many of them have extensive knowledge of suppliers, which means that they might be able to hire a marquee or organise the flowers, for example, for a more competitive price than you could. In addition, they know which suppliers are reliable.

Before you sign a contract with any wedding organiser make sure you read the small print and know exactly what the company's terms are. Some charge a flat fee of about £400 to £500, while others will charge a percentage fee. As the average wedding (including the honeymoon) costs about £10,000 the latter could be much more expensive.

If you choose to organise the wedding yourself you will find a good deal of information and advice, as well as numerous advertisements in the many wedding magazines. If you can visit one of the big wedding shows, held at exhibition centres, you will also find plenty of ideas and useful contacts there.

The following chapters describe how to organise your wedding yourself and should help you to avoid pitfalls. Even if you are employing the services of a wedding organiser, the information in this book will enable you to offer ideas and to keep track of the whole operation.

Breaking off the engagement

However upset and embarrassed you may be about breaking off an engagement, remember that it is easier to unpick a wedding than it is to unravel a marriage. Feeling a little uncertain that you are doing the right thing is far from unusual as the wedding approaches; almost everyone suffers from last-minute nerves or the urge to run away from the pressure. But if your doubts are more serious and persist even during the enjoyable parts of the preparations, it would be far better to talk over your fears and halt the proceedings, if only for a short period of time.

If you do decide to break off the engagement, inform relatives and friends quietly; you do not need to give an explanation. If you published an announcement in a newspaper you should place a notice of cancellation, which simply states your names and that the wedding will no longer take place.

An engagement to marry is no longer a legally binding contract, and the man cannot demand the return of the engagement ring. However, it is usual and courteous for the woman to at least offer to return it, allowing her fiancé to decide whether or not to accept it. The same offer should apply to anyone who has already sent a wedding gift.

Timetable

2

The peak wedding season is from April to September, and churches, photographers, florists, caterers, hotels, marquees and so on can get booked up months in advance. If you plan to marry between October and March you will not have to plan so far ahead.

Below is a timetable of what tasks need to be done when. However, as all weddings are different, no two lists of priorities are quite the same. Six to nine months should be adequate preparation time.

Soon after your engagement

- decide whether the wedding will be formal or informal
- decide, with both sets of parents, who is going to pay for what
- work out your budget (and stick to it)
- work out how many guests you can afford to invite and make a guest list
- choose the locations for the ceremony and the reception, find out the dates on which they are available, then book them
- choose the best man, chief bridesmaid/matron of honour, bridesmaids and page boys
- select and book a photographer and/or video company
- select and book the florist

- select and book the cars (one for the bride and her father and one for the bridesmaids and the bride's mother; possibly a third car for the groom and best man)
- select and book the caterers and any staff (for a reception in a private house)
- select and book a toastmaster (if you are having one)
- order your wedding cake or make your own
- book entertainment for the reception
- book the honeymoon
- find or order a wedding dress and head-dress
- choose attendants' clothes
- discuss the details for the reception.

Four to six months before

- order the wedding invitations (printing usually takes two to four weeks)
- arrange a wedding list for gifts (so that it is ready when you send your invitations out)
- confirm with the minister the dates of the banns and the details of the wedding
- decide on the form of service and the hymns you want if you are having a church wedding
- book organist and choir/soloist for the ceremony, if applicable
- book the hotel/B&B for the wedding night
- apply for visas, if needed for your honeymoon
- choose men's formal wear
- consider arranging wedding insurance (see Chapter 14).

Two to three months before

- send out invitations, with directions, map and accommodation list (usually six to nine weeks before the wedding)
- check off each acceptance or refusal
- agree food and drink menu with the caterers
- buy wedding ring(s)
- buy each other wedding gifts (optional)
- buy presents for best man and attendants
- arrange a date for a wedding rehearsal, if necessary
- (men) book morning suits if hiring (allow six weeks)
- buy shoes for the wedding (before your first wedding dress fitting so that you can try your dress on with the right ensemble) and wear them in the house so they are comfortable on the day
- have first wedding-dress fitting
- shop for trousseau
- consult beautician and hairdresser and try out different looks so both you and the hairdresser/beautician are clear about what has to be done on the day
- decide which pieces of luggage you will use for going away
- if possible, have any vaccinations needed for the honeymoon. Some can make you feel unwell so do not leave them to the last minute
- check or apply for your passport or arrange for a post-dated name change, if required (see page 20–21).

One month before

- check that guests who have failed to reply have received their invitations
- start a wedding present thank-you list – make sure you record exactly who gave you what
- arrange accommodation for guests travelling long distances
- confirm final arrangements for the flowers for the wedding venue, the reception, the bride, the mother of the bride, the bridesmaids and buttonholes for the bride's father, the groom, best man and ushers
- make a seating plan if you have planned a sit-down meal at the reception
- arrange music with the organist, if applicable
- confirm the date of the rehearsal
- prepare a newspaper announcement if applicable
- (chief bridesmaid and best man, usually) make arrangements for the stag and hen nights, which should be at least a week before the wedding
- book a manicure for the day before and a hair and/or make-up appointment for the day
- check that everyone in the wedding party has the correct attire
- have final wedding-dress fitting
- advise bank etc. of change of address and name.

One week before

- decorate cake (if it is home-made)
- wrap the gifts for the attendants and best man

- (bridegroom) place correct fees for the minister, organist, choir, bell-ringers and church heating in cash in marked envelopes and give these to the best man, together with keys for going-away car on the day
- pack the honeymoon luggage and check the honeymoon tickets
- have wedding rehearsal
- arrange for an appropriate person to take home the bride's dress and accessories after the wedding. The best man should take charge of the groom's clothes and, if they are hired, return them
- review the seating plan and prepare place cards
- confirm final number of guests to caterer.

The day before

- if you are using your car to go on your honeymoon, make sure it has petrol, oil, water and is in perfect running order
- pack going-away clothes and if possible have the suitcase delivered to the reception venue
- give the best man and attendants their presents
- (bride) have manicure.

On the day

- sleep late (if you can) and have a leisurely bath and a good breakfast
- allow yourself plenty of time to get dressed. If not using a hairstylist/beautician, the bride should do her hair and make-up slowly and carefully, adding veil and head-dress afterwards.

Changing your surname

Brides do not have to change their surnames when they get married. However, you may find that it makes life a little easier when you are making joint arrangements of a social, legal or financial nature.

You may prefer to keep your maiden name for work purposes. However, if your job involves a lot of travel be sure to let your employer know if you intend to change your bank or passport details.

If you do decide to change your name, you will need to amend a number of documents and contact a number of organisations. Do not panic: most can be done several weeks after the wedding when you have more time. However, some organisations may ask for sight of your marriage certificate.

The following are the most important organisations and people to contact: employer, bank, building society, insurance companies, credit-card companies, passport office, Inland Revenue, DSS, DVLC (for change of driver's licence and vehicle registration documents), GP, dentist.

If you are going abroad on your honeymoon and wish to travel abroad in your married name you will need to obtain a post-dated passport. Pick up leaflet PD1, form PD2 and form C from your main post office (for amending your existing passport). Those applying for a passport for the first time and those whose passport is no longer valid will need leaflet PD1, form PD2 and form A. If you are changing your surname on your passport after you are married you need to pick up leaflet PD1 and form PD2.

Allow at least one month for the application to be processed and up to three months if applying between February and June. Finally, check that the name on your passport and on your travel documents is the same. If you do not have time to amend your passport before you go on your honeymoon you must take your marriage certificate with your existing passport.

(The consulates of some countries do not grant visas on post-dated passports, passports amended with post-dated effect or passports in the woman's maiden name accompanied by the marriage certificate. Check with the relevant consulate in advance.) You can always travel with your passport in your maiden name, but remember to make sure that your tickets are in your maiden name too.

Principal Players

3

Think carefully before assigning these important roles: make sure that they are offered to people who are confident they can both enjoy and make a success of the duties.

Best man

The groom usually decides who will be the best man, and whoever he asks will be required to assist him before, during and after the wedding. Traditionally, the job is offered to the groom's closest unmarried male relative or friend. Ideally, the best man should be an excellent organiser and a trusty time-keeper who can be relied upon to stay sober on the day and offer a shoulder to lean on throughout the whole proceedings.

His responsibilities include:

- helping the groom to choose any ushers
- confirming all arrangements by liaising with the bride's family
- paying the clergyman/bell-ringers/organist/registrar on behalf of the groom
- organising transport and parking arrangements
- taking delivery of order-of-service sheets and buttonholes
- hiring clothes for himself, the groom and ushers
- arranging a stag night
- attending the wedding rehearsal

PRINCIPAL PLAYERS

- writing and making a speech
- taking charge of wedding ring(s)
- ensuring the groom arrives on time
- looking after the guests at the reception
- introducing the speeches, toasts and reading any telegrams at the reception
- ensuring any luggage is in the honeymoon vehicle
- returning all hired clothes.

Ushers

Chosen by the groom, they are usually members of either family or old friends of the couple. On the day, the ushers arrive about an hour early to look out for the first few guests. How many you have depends on the size of your wedding. Ushers:

- stand at the door of the place of the ceremony to hand out service sheets
- direct or show guests to their seats
- assist any guests with young children, and elderly or disabled guests, and take special care to escort principal guests to their seats.

Chief bridesmaid and bridal attendants

Chosen by the bride, they are traditionally unmarried female members of the bride's family or close circle of friends. If a married woman is chosen, she is known as the matron of honour. Page boys are often young family members or sons of the bride's best friends. On the day they follow the bridesmaids up the aisle, wait at the chancel steps and leave with them after the ceremony. At the reception, they will be expected to hand out slices of cake, following the cutting ceremony.

Bridesmaids are responsible for the following:

- assisting with selecting their own outfits and attending dress, shoe and head-dress fittings
- setting up the hen party
- helping the bride dress for the day and carry out any other tasks with which she may need help.

The chief bridesmaid is responsible for the other bridesmaids and should work in tandem with the bride's mother. She must:

- attend to the bride's dress and train on arriving at the church
- hold the bride's bouquet during the service and help her as she leaves for the reception
- assist the best man in welcoming guests at the reception.

Finally, the bride may ask the chief bridesmaid to help her as she prepares to leave the reception. This may involve taking charge of the dress once the bride has got changed into her going-away outfit.

Wedding Stationery

4

A formal wedding requires a formal invitation, whereas an informal wedding allows you the opportunity to design something original. Whatever you decide, all wedding invitations have one thing in common – they are a request from the host for the guest to attend the marriage of two people at a certain place and time on a given date, usually followed by a reception.

The formal wedding invitation

This should be printed or engraved on good-quality white or cream paper. The format is an upright, folded card measuring 14 × 18cm (5½ × 7in). You can choose from three different types of printing: engraving (or die stamping), thermographic printing and flat printing (the cheapest option). Engraving is traditional and still looks best as it gives the lettering a raised and embossed appearance but it is expensive (because a printing plate has to be made). Thermographic printing produces a similar result to that of engraving but is cheaper and not quite as smart. As its name suggests, flat printing produces lettering that is not raised; it looks like the lettering that is produced by a word processor. Ask your printer, stationer or department-store stationery section to show you examples of each. The wording appears on one side only. Black lettering is usual, although silver is an option.

Whatever format you decide upon, you should follow the set wording and layout for traditional cards:

>*Mr and Mrs Mark Baxter*
>*request the pleasure of*
>*your company/*
>*request the honour of*
>*your presence at the marriage*
>*of their daughter*
>*Alice*
>*to Mr Edward Holland*
>*at St Mary's Church, Lymington*
>*on (day, date, month, year)*
>*at (time)*
>*and afterwards at*
>*(reception location)*

RSVP
(parents'/hosts' address)

Another option would be to say:

>*Mr and Mrs Mark Baxter*
>*request the pleasure of/*
>*the company of*
>*(Name of guest(s), filled in by hand)*
>*...*
>*at the marriage of their daughter*

Alternative wordings
Even if the bride's parents are divorced, one of them has died or either has remarried, the same basic rule applies – the host sends the invitation. The announce-

ment should make it clear how the hosts and the bride are related to each other, i.e. 'his daughter', 'their daughter' etc.

Below are alternative wordings that follow the traditional style.

The bride's mother as host:

> *Mrs Richard Thorne*
> *requests the pleasure of*
> *your company at the marriage*
> *of her daughter...*

If the bride's mother is divorced, she uses her forename, Mrs Louisa Thorne; if she has remarried she uses her new husband's name, Mrs James Wallace. A widow usually keeps her husband's name, Mrs Patrick Matthews.

The bride's father as host:

> *Mr David Lloyd*
> *requests the pleasure of*
> *your company at the marriage*
> *of his daughter...*

The bride's divorced parents, neither having remarried, as hosts:

> *Mr David Lloyd and Mrs Katherine Lloyd*
> *request the pleasure of*
> *your company at the marriage*
> *of their daughter...*

The bride's divorced parents, the mother having remarried, as hosts:

> *Mr David Lloyd and Mrs James Wallace*
> *request the pleasure of*
> *your company at the marriage*
> *of their daughter...*

The bride's mother and stepfather as hosts:

> *Mr and Mrs James Wallace*
> *request the pleasure of*
> *your company at the marriage*
> *of her daughter...*

The bride's father and stepmother as hosts:

> *Mr and Mrs David Lloyd*
> *request the pleasure of*
> *your company at the marriage*
> *of his daughter...*

The bride as host:

> *Miss Sally Lloyd*
> *requests the pleasure of*
> *your company at her marriage to...*

The bride and groom as hosts:

> *Mr Adam Jackson and Miss Sally Lloyd*
> *request the pleasure of*
> *your company*
> *at their marriage*

Continental Europeans and members of the practising Jewish community send cards in the names of both sets of parents. For example:

> *Mr and Mrs John Collins*
> *request the pleasure of*
> *your company at the marriage*
> *of their daughter*
> *Annemarie*
> *to Matthew, son of Dr and Mrs Owen...*

A service of blessing can follow a marriage at a register office. The invitations should read as follows:

> *Mr and Mrs John Collins*
> *request the pleasure of your company*
> *at the Blessing of the Marriage*
> of their daughter
> Annemarie

Informal invitations

Informal invitations are the same as formal ones in as much as the host invites the guest to the wedding.

However, you will have more choice in what you say and how you say it. You may want to design your own wedding invitation using special wording or a sketch or photograph of yourselves or the wedding venue.

If the bride's parents are the hosts, the invitation could read:

Mr and Mrs John Collins
invite you to/have much pleasure
in inviting you to the marriage of their daughter
Annemarie
to Matthew Owen
at ...
on (day, date, month, year) at (time)
at RSVP address

The bride and groom are the hosts:

Annemarie Collins and Matthew Owen
(or Annemarie and Matthew)
invite you to their wedding
at ....
on (day, date, month, year) at (time)
at RSVP address

A good department store or large stationers should have several books of examples for you to look through. As a rough guide, for engraved invitations on 14 × 18cm (5½ × 7in) folded card you could expect to pay in a department store £108 for the first 25 invitations (most of the cost is creating the printing plate);

150 invitations cost £345 and 200 cost £375. For thermographic printing, the cost of 25 invitations on 8 × 6in double card is £84; 150 invitations cost £157 and 200 cost £186.

Check with the printer that envelopes are included with your order and that you will be sent a proof so that you can check the wording carefully. Look for the following:

- is the invitation worded correctly?
- do the lines fall in the correct places?
- do the day of the week and the date match?
- are all names including the venues for ceremony and reception spelled correctly?
- is the address complete and correct?
- is the punctuation correct?
- is the paper the colour you chose?
- is the style of lettering the one you asked for?

Addressing invitations

If you are sending an invitation to a husband and wife and their children live at home you need send only one. Their names should be written on the top left-hand corner or filled in the space provided. Parents should assume that the invitation is for them alone if their children's names are not specified. All envelopes should be hand-written and addressed with the correct full name and rank or title of the guest.

Sending the invitations

Take time to check the guest list with both sides of the family – any oversights on this will be remembered forever afterwards. Enclose a route map or parking instructions and a list of accommodation as appropriate. Ideally, you should post the invitations six to eight weeks before the ceremony.

Order-of-service sheets

Traditionally, the front of the service sheet will feature the name of the church and the time and date of the ceremony. The names of the bride and groom appear below, either as initials or forenames or in full. The bride's name is printed on the left and the groom's is on the right. All verses, hymns, prayers and responses are printed inside. As a rule of thumb, order one sheet for every guest plus a dozen extra in case of damage or unexpected arrivals.

You do not have to have service sheets printed. With most denominations, couples can choose to use the set order of service found in most prayer books, and the congregation can sing from hymn books.

Sample layout of service sheet

The procession: Arrival of the Queen of Sheba (Handel)

Introduction
Hymn: Jerusalem
(the whole text should be printed here)

The marriage between
Miss Grace Tulaman
and
Mr Rex Wilson

Hymn: Love Divine All Loves Excelling
(the whole text again)
The Sermon
The Signing of the Register

Hymn: Amazing Grace
(the whole text)

The Recessional: La Rejouissance, Music for the Royal Fireworks (Handel)

Copyright on hymns

Check whether your chosen hymns are under copyright. If any is, you will need to seek permission from the copyright holder to reprint it in your order of service sheets. Details of copyright can be found either in the acknowledgements at the front of the hymn book or under the paragraph on copyright. The vast majority are copyright-free, but if permission is required the relevant address will be printed. Some copyright owners may ask for a small fee, while most will settle for a brief written acknowledgement beside the hymn in question.

DRESS AND ACCESSORIES

Choosing an outfit in which you will look and feel right on the day is one of the most important, enjoyable decisions you will make in the run-up to the ceremony. If you are lucky enough to know what you are looking for, the only issue is finding it or having it made for you. Otherwise, start your search by taking a careful look at every wedding picture you see – in magazines, local newspapers, photographers' windows and advertisements.

Another good starting point is to consider the dress in the context of the ceremony. A grand church wedding calls for a traditional long white or off-white dress. As most guests will be looking at the back of the dress during the ceremony you should think about having details like covered buttons or a sash to hide any seams at the waist.

If you are getting married later in life or for the second time you could opt for a smart suit or day dress in a special fabric, such as lace or silk. Any of the near-white colours such as oyster, ivory, cream or magnolia – or a pastel shade – look bridal. There are no set rules as to what you should wear if you are marrying in a non-religious setting. You could wear a smart suit or dress, but it is also quite acceptable to wear a long white dress at a register office.

Alternatives to Buying

If buying a ready-made wedding dress is beyond your budget, you could hire one, have one made by a dressmaker or make it yourself.

Hiring

You may be able to hire a dress from a high-street department store or specialist shop, although fewer shops are now offering this service than in the past. Check:

- that the dress will be available on your wedding day
- that it is possible to make minor alterations to it
- what the alternatives are if it is damaged during a previous rental or otherwise becomes unavailable
- how many days the cost of the hire covers
- whether the fee includes insurance against damage and the cost of cleaning.

Hire costs about £300. You will probably have to give about twelve weeks' notice and will be able to collect the dress two days before the wedding. However, it usually has to be returned two days after.

Making your dress yourself/having it made for you

If you are going to make the dress yourself, think carefully about your skills and expertise. Unless you have settled on a very simple, straightforward style, taking on the role of dressmaker can be unneccessarily stressful at a time when you have a lot to think about and organise. In addition, a complicated creation will require more material than a simple one, making the dress much more expensive.

The price of materials can vary tremendously (see below), so it is worth shopping around: compare prices over the phone. You could even ask the shops to send you swatches.

If you are having your dress made you must also consider whether you have time for the several fittings that a professional dressmaker will require.

Price guide

Duchess satin (140cm wide) – a heavy, semi-stiff 100 per cent pure silk fabric – ranges from £40 to £49 per metre. Medium-weight 100 per cent pure silk (112cm wide) ranges from £15 to £47 per metre. Silk organza (110cm wide) – lightweight, semi-transparent 100 per cent silk – ranges from £9.50 to £12.50 per metre.

Always check the width of cloth your pattern requires before purchasing your fabric. Bring your pattern with you and show it to the shop assistant before he or she cuts the cloth.

Borrowing

Once worn, a wedding dress often becomes a burden for married women. Many keep them forever and for no real purpose. So if your mother's wedding dress appeals, for example, why not tick off two of the requirements from the saying 'something old, something new, something borrowed, something blue'?

Second-hand

A third option is to buy a second-hand dress. Some shops specialise in selling them, and you will find advertisements for these at the back of wedding magazines and in your local telephone directories. Charity shops can also be a good hunting ground. Some people sell their dress privately; you will find advertisements in *Loot* (an advertisements newspaper sold regionally throughout the UK) and in the classified sections of magazines and local newspapers. Second-hand dresses can be bought for about half of the original cost or less. Many of these dresses have not been worn at all and the rest have been worn only once.

SHOES

White or even pale-coloured shoes are often in short supply in the winter months, so if your wedding is planned for that time of year, buy them in the spring or summer. As you will be on your feet for most of your wedding day, your shoes must be comfortable. Before the wedding make sure they have stretched to fit your feet. Wear them around the house with a pair of thin cotton socks and also try rubbing the soles with sandpaper or a metal-bristled suede brush. This will help ensure that you do not slip on the day. New tights or stockings will grip your legs better if they have been washed once. Buy two pairs in case you ladder them as you are dressing for your wedding.

Head-dresses

There are many different types of bridal head-dress. Currently faux-gemstone tiaras are popular but you could choose flowers (see page 47). Try on a variety of head-dresses and choose one that goes with your dress and veil.

Veils

Veils vary in price, usually depending on the material (silk tulle, nylon tulle, lace and organza, for example) and how ornate they are. Some are completely plain, some have beads scattered on them, while others have scalloped edges. They can be long or short. The general rule is that if you have a train you wear a full-length veil, which is about a foot longer than the train, and if you do not have a train you wear a short veil. It is not considered appropriate for divorced women to wear a veil.

Glasses

Glasses can look a bit incongruous with a veil so try pinning the veil back off your face with a bridal hair-clip or comb. Keep the neckline of your dress fairly plain, and, if wearing a shade of white, wear light spectacle frames. Tell the photographer in advance if you want to wear glasses for your formal photos so he/she can plan the best positions to avoid glare on the lenses.

Photographs and Videos   6

Before selecting a photographer try to visit several studios. This will give you the chance to compare the styles and packages available and see the standard and quality of each photographer's work. Personal recommendations are invaluable, but many studios are featured in the phone book or may even have an office on the high street. Make an initial phone call to find out whether he or she is available on your wedding day. Many reputable photographers are booked for up to a year in advance.

When you visit each studio you should find out the following:

- **is the photographer's portfolio a true reflection of his or her work?** A good portfolio should reflect the fact that every wedding is unique. A balance should be struck between the formal and the informal. Ask to see samples of work that range from the start of the wedding to the end, rather than just the highlights. You should aim to get an idea of how your wedding will look through the lens
- **who is going to take the photographs on the day?** Ensure that you view this person's work and not just the studio book comprising that of several photographers
- **how does he or she intend to cover the key shots?** Make sure that you are happy with the way the pho-

tographer deals with the key group photographs; will he take a mixture of formal and informal pictures? Do you like the way the groups in the photographs in the studio albums are put together? Is the photographer flexible enough to do exactly as you want?

- **what insurance does the photographer offer?** Check what business cover your photographer possesses and the implication to you for compensation. While it is in the photographer's interest to provide the best possible service, there is always a chance that the film can be damaged or even lost
- **can you work together on the day?** Your photographer will be a major presence throughout your wedding. Try to take stock of his character. Is he helpful or bossy, unobtrusive or fixed in his ways? No matter how skilled and evocative his work, a photographer who irritates everyone could cast a cloud over your entire day.

Negotiating a package

Having talked to a number of photographers, you will have an idea of the range of packages on offer. Many combinations are available. For example, you may prefer your final portfolio to feature some black and white or even sepia-coloured prints, in which case check that your photographer can include these in the package. You might also wish to have photographs of various sizes. Many estimates will include an album and a number of finished shots; some photographers will quote for their time on the day and their prints will be extra; others will charge only for prints and not for their time. Alternatively, a photographer may charge for time only but offer unlimited prints. Some packages include parent albums (smaller versions of the main album), while others offer them as an optional extra. Most photographers will show you a wide range of photograph albums to choose from. They might be leather or plastic and come in a range of colours, with a variety of borders for the photographs (rectangle, square, round or even heart-shaped).

Counting the cost

For a professional photographer expect to pay in the region of £150 upwards for a small register office wedding. This can soar to £1,000 or more if you decide to have all the trimmings, which might include a prepared storyboard of the shots to be covered throughout your day, more than one photographer, unlimited prints and an album.

Hidden extras

When finalising the deal, check for any extra charges such as development and delivery of proofs and VAT.

VIDEO

Having a video made of the wedding is becoming increasingly popular. You might like to show your wedding video as part of your entertainment at the reception. Many photographers can recommend or even offer a video service. Follow the same selection proce-

PHOTOGRAPHS AND VIDEOS

dure recommended for choosing a photographer. You should ask to see previous work and feel comfortable with the operator. While any reputable video service will provide insurance, some also offer a customer dissatisfaction clause. Here, financial compensation may be available if an independent arbitration panel judges the final product to be of an inferior standard to that agreed in your contract. Below is a price guideline:

- £450 – video (two copies) from the bride's house until the first dance at the reception, plus music of your choice, the copyright licence and photographs taken from the video
- £350–400 – the same package but ending after the speeches at the reception
- £250 and under – the same package but ending after the ceremony.

Flowers

7

Planning your flowers is another of those tasks that should be done while considering the scale and type of wedding you are having. The groom is traditionally responsible for paying for the mothers' corsages, all men's buttonholes, the bride's and bridesmaids' flowers, while the bride's parents pay for the rest. Agree your budget before you visit the florist and stick to it. Flowers for a winter wedding are about a third more expensive than those for a summer wedding.

Choosing your florist

A skilled friend or relation or even the bride herself could arrange the flowers. But unless the style you require is fairly simple and informal it is probably wise to leave it to a professional florist.

Florists can get very booked up in the summer months so phone a few to check availability before visiting the shop. Make an appointment, and, if possible, take along samples of your dress fabric and sketches of your dress and any attendants' outfits.

Take any magazine photographs of arrangements you admire for your bouquet or the wedding or reception venue. If your order is likely to be considerable ask the florist to visit you at home so he or she can appraise your personal style and tastes. The florist may also wish to visit the wedding and reception venues. Ask to see the florist's portfolio.

If you are having only bouquets and buttonholes make sure the florist knows whether you plan to pick them up on the day or want them delivered.

Choosing your flowers

Listed below are the flowers of which you will need a selection.

Wedding party

- bride's bouquet
- bride's head-dress if appropriate
- bridesmaids' bouquets
- bridesmaids' head-dresses if appropriate
- mothers' corsages
- groom's, fathers', best man's and ushers' buttonholes.

Church

- altar
- pulpit
- lectern
- windowsills
- font
- columns
- church entrance
- chancel steps
- pew ends.

Synagogue

- *chuppah*

You will need to obtain the minister's/rabbi's permission before decorating the church/synagogue. Some ministers prefer the altar to be left unadorned so that the Cross is the focal point.

The minister may be able to suggest someone who helps with the church flowers every week to give you advice about the best floral arrangement for the church. For a small donation he or she might even be available to help on the day. If another couple is getting married in the church on the same day you may wish to consider liaising with them and sharing the cost of the church flowers. The minister/rabbi should be able put you in touch with them.

Reception

- entrance
- buffet table
- dining tables
- cake
- cake table.

The bride's bouquet

Some brides prefer not to have a bouquet at all – traditionally, if you opt to wear a hat rather than veil, flowers are considered to be unnecessary.

White flowers interspersed with variegated foliage is the most traditional choice but is not always advisable. Not all whites are the same shade. Natural white flowers set against the bluey-white of perhaps a part-synthetic dress would make the flowers look yellowy and even drab. A subtle selection of colours with white can be used to great effect.

You could choose a countrified posy or a basket of flowers, a stunning stem of lilies or a bouquet made up without flowers. Depending on the time of year, you might consider foliage, wheat sheafs, holly berries, ivy, grasses and ferns.

Expect to pay approximately £50 upwards, depending on the time of year and choice of flowers. A shower bouquet, with the flowers cascading down is more complex and starts at about £95.

The bride's head-dress
Flowers always make a beautifully classic head-dress. You can choose from a variety of styles, including a whole or half circlet, specially decorated hair combs or slides or a few tiny flowers threaded randomly through your hair. Before coming to any decision discuss your ideas with your hairdresser for the day. Take care to choose flowers that will not wilt too quickly if the weather is likely to be hot. Even the heat from your head can make a floral head-dress droop. Fresh-flower head-dresses cost from £35.

Buttonholes and corsages
Expect to pay £3 per buttonhole and between £7.50 and £10 per corsage. Red or white carnations are traditional for the buttonholes but not together as it can be considered bad luck (symbolising blood and bandages). A sprig of heather is perceived to be good luck but a single or double rosebud in your chosen colours are currently the most popular choice. You should provide pins to attach the flowers to dresses and jackets. Some summer dress fabrics are very light and delicate so check what is being worn before deciding on a large, heavy, ornate arrangement.

The groom's mother's flowers and all buttonholes should be sent directly to the wedding venue on the morning of the wedding; the best man should receive and distribute them. Check that he is aware of this duty.

Transport

8

Most brides who have a formal white wedding in a church/synagogue hire at least one chauffeur-driven car. While this is not absolutely necessary, it has many advantages. Most hired cars used for weddings are elegant and roomy, allowing the bride to travel in comfort and style and to arrive at the church unruffled. It is usual to hire two cars.

The bride and her father travel from the house to the church in one, and the other takes the bride's mother and bridesmaids or other close family. After the wedding the bride and groom leave for the reception in the first car, and the second takes the parents of the bride and possibly bridesmaids or any attendants. The best man should ensure that all the wedding party, groom's parents, all grandparents and close family have reliable transport to the reception and also, with the help of the ushers, make sure that the guests can get there without difficulty.

Choosing your transport

Cars are still the most popular form of wedding transport. They range from white London taxis (hackney carriages) to American Cadillacs, vintage Rolls-Royces or Daimlers.

Horse-drawn carriages, with optional liveried coachmen and footmen or pageboys, or closed carriages, with heated interiors for winter, are also available.

The more complicated the transport arrangements, the earlier you should start organising and confirming them. Do not forget to check whether such details as white ribbons on the wedding cars or rosettes for the horses are included in the price quoted. It is courteous to tip drivers, grooms or footmen but not expected. This is another duty for the best man, so arrange it with him beforehand.

If you want a Cinderella-style coach with horses you should book well in advance as popular summer dates can be booked up for two years or more.

Most companies will be able to offer a choice of colour of the horses. Although this cannot be guaranteed they will do their best to make the ones you have chosen available. Expect to pay in the region of £400 to £800, depending on the number of horses, distance and choice of carriage.

Wedding cars

Once again, a personal recommendation is the best source for finding a reliable car-hire company but your telephone directory or a specialist wedding magazine will provide a good starting point. Again, booking well in advance is strongly advisable.

A car-hire company should be able to quote for a tailor-made package to suit your requirements. Remember:

- visit the car-hire company and inspect the fleet of cars
- ensure that the car you see is the car you will get, not a similar one or different model. Have this in writing
- ask if the car is a genuine vintage or veteran vehicle or classic car and not 'in the style of' a traditional model. A vintage car is one made between 1917 and

1930. Older veteran cars are divided into two classes: those made before 1916 and those made before 1905. Kit cars are made up from parts of other cars and although they can look effective they should be substantially cheaper to hire than an original model
- look at the general condition of the car: the tyres, leather seating, head lining, woodwork, rust marks, smooth paintwork and so on
- ask if any matching ribbons or silk flowers are included in the price
- make sure you have a written guarantee that the car(s) you book will be used only for your wedding on that day and the company will not try to fit you in before, after or during another ceremony, however near it is to your own

TRANSPORT

- check that the chauffeur is included in the price
- check that a large umbrella is supplied with the car (preferably a cream or white one)
- practice getting in and out of the car wearing similar clothes to your wedding outfit – not jeans
- a white or cream natural silk dress can look dull or even disappear against brilliant white paintwork. Ask to see how the car looks in photographs and get advice from a professional photographer
- in modern cars you are required by law to wear a seatbelt in the front and back, but vintage and veteran cars and some classic models have them only in the front or not at all. If the car was genuinely manufactured before the seatbelt laws were enforced, you are exempt from wearing them. This might be an important consideration if you have a particularly large dress or one that creases easily.

Every wedding will require a different service but expect to pay £150-plus.

Parking arrangements

Parking provision at both the place of marriage and the reception venue needs to be checked in advance, particularly if either or both venues are in the centre of a busy town. Check whether both the wedding venue and the reception venue have large car parks. If they do not you should investigate nearby parking facilities and include details, possibly with a map, with your wedding invitations.

Wedding cake

9

The wedding cake, though not compulsory, is still considered a focal point of the reception. Traditionally, it is a rich fruitcake, with two to four tiers that have been iced and decorated. However, a single-tier sponge or a large iced chocolate confection are equally acceptable.

If you decide to keep the top tier for your first child's christening you must choose a fruitcake otherwise it will not stay fresh. After the wedding day wrap the cake in tinfoil and place it in the freezer; this way it will stay in perfect condition for years.

The home-made option

A rich fruitcake improves in taste and texture if it has been given time to mature. If possible, allow three months for the preparation and decoration.

You will need about 2.25kg/5lb of cake for every 45 to 50 guests. If you plan to keep the top tier, calculate the weight required from the lower tiers only. Ingredients for a simple three-tiered wedding cake cost about £45 if purchased from a supermarket.

You may decide that making the cake yourself is an unnecessary chore on top of an already hectic schedule. But if you have a competent cook in your family or circle of friends you could ask him or her. A home-made cake can save more than half the cost of a professionally-commissioned cake.

The professional option

Ideally, a many-tiered cake should be ordered months in advance. Look in your local telephone directory for an appropriate confectioner. Otherwise, bridal magazines or personal recommendations are a possible starting point. Shop around: prices begin at about £150 for a simple three-tiered cake. Remember to ask how many guests this will feed, bearing in mind you may wish to keep the top tier for your first child's christening.

Ask to see a catalogue of photographs showing cakes the confectioner has made. Any good confectioner should also be happy to provide a sample of real cake to ensure you like the taste. Establish a delivery time in advance of the day and confirm all the details in writing. If you have ordered a tiered cake, ask the following questions:

- **how will the cake be delivered?** Confirm that each tier will be packed in a separate box to avoid damage
- **who will construct each layer?** The caterer or the confectioner?
- **are the pillars and display tray included in the final price?**
- **are the top decorations provided?** Many confectioners offer a wide range of adornments
- **is the confectioner insured against loss or damage of the cake prior to delivery or during transit?**

The quick option

If you do not have much time and would like to keep costs down you could buy plain, iced fruit cake from a supermarket and construct your own tiered wedding cake. Prices range from £6 to 26 per tier.

Music

Well-chosen music during the ceremony helps to create the mood of your wedding. Do not leave the choice to the last minute. If you are having a religious wedding try not to let the organist make the decision for you, although he or she will be able to advise you.

Music for a church wedding

You will need to think about music for the entrance of the bride, some hymns, music to be played or sung during the signing of the register and for the recessional. It is courteous, and sometimes necessary, to consult your minister before making your final decision. He or she will not make the decision for you but will be able to offer you guidance.

There are no set rules about the number of hymns you should have, although the standard is three. Traditionally, the first is played at the beginning of the service, the second after the marriage itself and the final hymn after you have signed the register. You may wish to have a choir to lead the congregation during the hymns and to sing during the service and the signing of the register, or a friend or a professional to sing or play an instrument at this point. You do not have to include any music during the service at all, and some ceremonies, such as Quaker marriages never have any.

Non-religious music
Some ministers may be happy for you to include a non-traditional tune, providing its style is in keeping with the gravity of the ceremony. Check beforehand.

Music for alternative ceremonies

If you are getting married in a non-church setting, you may want to include non-traditional music in your ceremony – perhaps choose something that reminds you of a special moment in your relationship or a tune that says something about you both. Your choice of venue may dictate the music you wish to play. While a register office may be equipped with a sound-system that you can use, you may find that some hotels or country houses have stricter policies regarding conduct during the ceremony.

Bells

A hearty peal of bells enhances any traditional church ceremony. If you wish to have the bells rung check with your minister that they are functioning and that ringers are available on the day. Bell-ringers require a fee and are paid in cash by the best man prior to the wedding. A peal of bells as you exit the church will cost about £30 to £60.

Gifts

11

Gifts are the traditional way for friends and relatives to help the bridal pair set up their home. Linen, china, glass, cutlery and home accessories are still popular as both of you will benefit from them.

As soon as you send out your invitations people will ask what you would like as a wedding present. While your wedding guests are not obliged to buy you a gift, most people feel it is a fitting way to mark the marriage. Here are some simple steps you can follow to ensure this wedding custom turns out well for all concerned.

One way to try to make sure that gifts are not duplicated is to make use of a wedding gift service run by one of the major stores. The procedure is quite straightforward and involves making a list of items you like in the shop. You should not feel that you have to choose everything from one store, however. In fact, most couples and guests prefer a list made up of gifts from different sources. Once you have made your selection, the list is then held by the shop (or shops) and shown to anyone who asks to see it. As the various items are chosen the store crosses them off the list and sends them to you. Some stores will hold all your gifts (if they have space) and deliver them after your honeymoon, while others make a weekly delivery.

If possible, you should have more items on the list than you actually expect to receive so that the last person to buy a present is not left without a choice. It is also courteous to select gifts from a broad price range so that every guest can pick something within their means.

If you prefer not to have a wedding gift list at a shop you should write a list and entrust it with one person (perhaps the bride's mother) whom the guests can consult. Be sure to give as much information as possible about make, colour and design etc. to your guests. The more specific you can be the better. The person who is looking after the list should check off the gifts as they are bought to avoid duplication. If the same present is accidentally purchased twice, most shops and stores will exchange gifts providing they have not been used.

You should not dispatch the list automatically but wait until you are asked for it. This allows guests to use their imagination to purchase something individual.

Thank-you letters

Whenever you receive a present, make a note of what it is, who sent it and when it arrived. You should send a hand-written thank-you letter for every gift you receive – even if it is from a close friend whom you have already thanked in person.

It is far easier to write a thank-you letter as each gift arrives, rather than letting them accumulate. When writing, try to be brief but be specific. It is possible for a shop to make a mistake and send you only two teacups when six were ordered and paid for. The person concerned will then have the opportunity to correct the mistake. If a gift comes from two or three people write to each one separately, but if you receive a gift from a large group – your colleagues at work, for example – then address one letter to the group as a whole.

Reception

12

The reception can be as simple or as elaborate as you like, depending on your taste and budget.

Choosing the venue

Your venue will depend on your budget and how many guests you wish to invite. Popular venues for a wedding reception are a local restaurant, a room in a pub, a hotel/country club, sports club, village hall, at home, or in a marquee in your garden. A rough estimate of the space required is about one square metre per person.

Before choosing a restaurant or hotel with which you are not familiar, visit it and have a meal there. Take note of general hygiene in the cloakrooms, standards of service and the quality of the food. Is the dining-room draughty or stuffy? Is there an efficient sound system? Is the atmosphere lively or sombre? Is it what you both want?

When visiting a possible venue, check for sufficient cloakrooms, toilets, facilities for any guests with disabilities, provision of seating for guests who may be frail or elderly and parking spaces. (These factors must also be considered if you decide to have your reception at home.)

Also consider the distance between the church or register office and the location of the reception. Try to choose a venue close to where the ceremony will take place. If this is impossible, remember to provide your guests with a detailed map and directions.

100 guests and over

If you are inviting one hundred or more guests to your reception you will need a substantial venue, such as a large hotel or restaurant, barn or stately home. You could also hire a marquee.

Marquees
While a suitable marquee is relatively easy to hire for entertaining a large number of guests, finding an appropriate open space to accommodate it is often much harder. If you have arranged to site your marquee in a private space such as your lawn you should tell your neighbours in advance about the crowd of guests, noise levels and increase in demand for parking. You must also think about the toilet facilities – as you may have to hire portable toilets along with your marquee.

Prices for a marquee for 100 and 150 guests

	100 guests	**150 guests**
marquee	20×60ft £220	40×80ft £440
lining	£170	£270
coconut matting	£110	£190
small dance floor	16×12ft £140	16×20ft £200
chandelier lighting	£60	£120
heating, if required	£60	£120

Extras
tables: trestles £3.00 each; 5ft round £5.00 each
chairs: white bistro £1.00 each; gilt £2.00
toilets: basic £70 per cubicle up to £400 for a luxury double unit.

All these estimates are pro rata and exclude VAT. Public liability is included.

A 25 per cent deposit will be requested at the time of booking, which is non-returnable. Prices are often cheaper if you book early.

50–100 guests

As a general rule, the smaller the number of guests invited to your reception, the greater the choice of venue. Most hotels or big country houses will be able to offer a function room and facilities that will accommodate 50–100 guests. A marquee in the host's garden, a smart pub or the village hall might also appeal.

Up to 50 guests

If you have fewer than 50 guests your range of options will be wider, from a restaurant to your own home. If you do have your reception at home, give uninvited neighbours advance notice as a matter of courtesy. Again, consider parking facilities, especially if parking permits are required.

CHOOSING A CATERER

Allow time to compare catering services and estimates. Good caterers tend to get booked up months in advance so try to book early (especially if the wedding is during the summer months). The best recommendation is word of mouth. If you do not know anything about the firms you have selected, ask them to send you references and always follow them up. The caterers will want to know:

- **the date and time of your reception**
- **where it is to be held** If it is in a village hall, for example, they will want to see what facilities are available
- **how many guests you expect**
- **your budget per head**
- **what kind of event you have in mind**
- **if any of your guests require special food** Some guests may have special dietary requirements so you might have to modify the set menu. Children's portions/meals should also be considered
- **if you wish them to supply champagne and wine** If you are supplying your own they will charge corkage (for opening and serving the wine)

Once you have arranged this verbally confirm it in writing. Remember to let your caterers know if there are any last-minute additions to your guest list. You must expect to pay for the number of guests confirmed, whether they appear or not.

Different independent caterers will probably offer very similar menus, but the prices can vary tremendously. Ask whether the price includes: tables and chairs; table linen; crockery and glasses; flowers or flower vases; cake stand and knife; staff such as waiters and waitresses; cloakroom attendants or a toastmaster.

If the party is to be held at a hall, private house or marquee make certain that the caterer understands that you will need them to clear up after the party as well as setting up before.

When choosing a menu, you may have to cater for a wide range of tastes, and it is prudent to include some vegetarian options. Confirm exactly what the basic price includes; you may be charged extra for bread, for example. Stick to your original budget. If you are having a buffet check that you are being charged per person and not per plate. Some caterers may charge for second helpings. Also check that you are not expected to pay for their staff to have a meal. Always ask if VAT is included and whether tips are expected in addition to the final fee.

Taking on the catering yourselves

This is the ideal solution if your budget is tight, particularly if family members help.

As you delegate tasks, make notes of who is doing what and when and keep a written record of any items you borrow from friends. You can hire cutlery, crockery and glasses from specialist firms. Enquire whether any of your neighbours have space in their freezers or whether they are able to assist with heating or warming up pre-prepared dishes on the day. Make sure that there are enough helpers available to undertake the following tasks: setting up the tables and decorations; laying out the food and drink; making final preparations; helping to serve the food, even at a buffet; clearing up afterwards. Choose food that is simple, fresh and in season, and needs little preparation.

Selecting drinks

If you have decided to hold your reception in a hotel or restaurant you will need to discuss with the management or wine waiter which wines you wish to be served. If you have opted to do the catering yourself, you will have to buy the alcohol. Champagne and wine are usually provided on a sale-or-return basis, while the glasses are sometimes offered free by the off-licence or wine merchant supplying the drinks. Be clear about the number and shape of glasses you require and be prepared for a small charge for breakages. (The off-licence or wine merchant should also be able to provide or recommend an ice supplier for the day.)

If you hire a venue for the reception privately (a village hall or stately home, for example) you will need to check that there is a licence to consume alcohol; if not, you can apply for a temporary (occasional) licence from the magistrates' court.

It is customary to offer your guests a drink as they arrive at the reception. Champagne, buck's fizz (champagne mixed with fresh orange juice) or sparkling wine are very welcoming, but red or white wine or a glass of sherry are also acceptable. If you are having a winter wedding you might like to serve mulled wine. Soft drinks should also be offered for non-drinkers, drivers and children. The choice of non-alcoholic drinks has vastly improved in recent years so you could serve alcohol-free wine or beer as well as the usual fruit juices, water and fizzy drinks.

Which drinks you choose for the rest of the reception will depend very much on your preferences and your knowledge of your guests. If the reception is held in the afternoon many people would probably relish a cup of tea at some point. The bride and groom are traditionally toasted with champagne. This, of course, depends on your budget, and a good-quality sparkling wine makes an adequate substitute at perhaps half the price.

Calculating the amount of drink required for your guests (to cover arrival and subsequent toasts) should be based on six glasses of wine or champagne per bottle, or twelve if you are serving buck's fizz. An average of half a bottle of wine per head is a realistic limit for the rest of the day's proceedings.

Toastmasters

It is not compulsory to hire a toastmaster, but if you do, his duties might be to announce: the arrival of each guest or couple; the start of lunch/dinner or buffet; the start of the speeches and toasts; the cutting of the cake.

A toastmaster's job is to oversee the running of the reception in a low-key, unobtrusive way. You can decide which duties you want him to fulfil and he should be able to conduct them with authority and style without being pompous. It is traditional for toastmasters to wear a scarlet tailcoat – but you can ask for black. Expect to pay about £200 for a professional. Remember that your best man can do all the jobs of a toastmaster.

The receiving line

Every wedding reception tends to follow a set pattern. Some couples have a receiving line as the guests arrive at the reception. This ensures that everyone has a chance to greet and congratulate the bride and groom. If you have a toastmaster he will call out the names of the guests in turn. The correct order for the receiving line is the bride's mother and father, the groom's mother and father, bride, groom, chief bridesmaid, best man.

Many people shorten this substantially in order to prevent guests having to queue. You might choose to have just the two of you in the receiving line or you could just circulate together to welcome each guest. Try not to spend too long with any one person and avoid being monopolised. This is not easy but it is important that you talk to every guest.

The seating plan

If the reception involves a sit-down meal the bridal couple sit with their families at the top table. The basic seating plan (from left to right).

- chief bridesmaid
- groom's father
- bride's mother
- groom
- bride
- bride's father
- groom's mother
- best man.

The line-up can vary but convention still has it that married couples (except for the bride and groom) do not sit next to each other at a formal reception. You could change the positions of the best man and chief bridesmaid or add a brother, sister or close relation as a partner for any unaccompanied member to even out the numbers. It would probably be wise as well as tactful to have place cards at the top table to avoid any delay or confusion when seating guests.

The toasts and speeches

The best man or toastmaster should keep on eye on the proceedings. He should judge when the majority of guests are near the end of their meal and stand up to invite the bride and groom to cut the cake. The toasts and speeches follow immediately after this.

Traditionally the bride's father, the groom and the best man each make a speech. Even at the most formal of weddings three or four speeches are plenty. However, there are no hard and fast rules on who may speak, and nowadays many brides also decide to address their guests.

Speakers should avoid drinking too much beforehand and try to keep calm and unflustered. Remember that yours is a well-disposed and receptive audience, ready and willing to be amused by your words. The old axiom 'if you can't be witty, be brief', is worth heeding when making a wedding speech.

The best man should end the speeches by reading some or all of the telemessages – if that is your wish. Finally, he can announce a toast to the bride and groom. At this point your guests stand up, raise their glasses and drink to your good health. If you are having a dance this is the time to take the lead on the dance floor.

The entertainment

You can choose any type of music, from classical or pop to jazz or country, for your reception but it should be light-hearted enough to appeal to a broad age group and never so loud as to irritate anyone. Be aware of the nature of the occasion and try to include some tunes for a younger or older generation.

Going away

At a suitable, pre-appointed time, the bride should change into her going-away outfit and meet her new husband at the door of the reception venue. (He may also change at this point if he is wearing a hired suit.) Here, the best man should assist the groom in every way possible, for example, by:

- taking charge of hired clothes
- seeing that the luggage is safely in the car

> ### Children
>
> While many people feel that weddings are a family occasion and that children should be invited and included in the celebrations, others do not. If you are worried about children getting bored or disrupting your wedding reception you might consider hiring an entertainer for an hour or two rather than not inviting them at all. Both parents and children might probably be very grateful for the opportunity to spend some time with their own peer group.
>
> Your local telephone directory should list children's entertainers such as clowns, magicians, story tellers, face painters etc. Some companies specialise in providing crêche facilities at weddings and will even supervise the children during the meal. The price depends on the ages and number of the children. Ideally, get a personal recommendation and ask for references, which should be followed up.

- checking with the groom that he has the tickets, money, keys and passports if you are going abroad.

Your guests should try to stay until you have departed, but if you are having a late dance or disco there is no need for everyone to wait. When your departure is imminent, the best man or toastmaster announces that you are 'going away', giving everyone the chance to rally round for your send-off. Keep your farewells fairly brief to prevent them getting too emotional. The bride should have her bridal bouquet with her so she can throw it into the crowd, if she wishes, before making her exit with her new husband.

CEREMONY   13

What happens during the ceremony depends on whether you are having a civil or religious wedding, and if it is religious, what denomination you are.

Church of England

Prior to the ceremony itself you should arrange to have a rehearsal of the wedding. If you are both working and cannot arrange a time during the day the minister might be able to set aside one evening. The bride's father, the best man and any attendants should also be there if possible. In addition, those reading at the ceremony and anyone performing might wish to practice in the church. There is no need to wear any special clothes other than everyday wear, but you should take notice of any steps or uneven flooring. The rehearsal provides the ideal opportunity for everyone to familiarise themselves with the order in which they will arrive at and depart from the church.

On the day, the groom and best man arrive about half an hour before the ceremony is due to start. When the guests arrive they are greeted by the ushers and shown where to sit. Shortly before the ceremony the bride's mother arrives with the bridesmaids (a few minutes before the bride herself).

The bride's family and friends sit on the left of the church and the groom's family and friends sit on the right. However, you do not have to stick to this tradition, especially if you have been together for a long time and know each other's friends equally well. The groom and best man wait in the top right-hand pew (nearest the altar). The bride walks up the aisle on the right-hand side of the person giving her away and is followed by her bridesmaids or attendants. When she reaches the chancel steps she hands her bouquet to one of her party (usually her chief bridesmaid or matron of honour), and the groom and best man move to the right hand of the altar to join her.

After the bride and groom have been pronounced man and wife, they and the minister sign the register in the vestry; this is witnessed by at least two adults. Make sure your witnesses are aware of this task beforehand – it is usual to ask your parents.

At the end of the ceremony the bridal party leaves the church in the following order:

Door

Bride	Groom
Bridesmaids	Pageboys
Chief Bridesmaid	Best Man
Bride's Mother	Groom's Father
Groom's Mother	Bride's Father

Altar

Church of Scotland, Church in Wales and Church of Ireland ceremonies are similar to that of the Church of England.

Civil

At the civil ceremony you can choose whether to arrive together or separately. Try not to arrive too early or too late as you risk getting caught up with another wedding. The registrar may want a brief word with you both to make sure all is in order before the ceremony. While this is happening your guests can take their places. The whole ceremony lasts 10–15 minutes. Civil weddings must not contain any religious elements, although you may ask permission to include some music and/or poems, and to embellish the vows, thereby making the ceremony more personal. After you have been declared man and wife you, two witnesses and the registrar sign the register. Check with the superintendent registrar in advance whether you may take photographs or use a video-recorder.

If you have a large number of guests you could consider having a civil wedding in a building approved for marriage by the local authority such as a hotel or stately home, a football ground etc. There are currently about 2,000 of these in England and Wales. A full list can be obtained from the Office for National Statistics.

Roman Catholic

The Roman Catholic ceremony can be conducted either with or without a nuptial mass (mass will not take place if one of you is not Christian). It is usual to have a rehearsal of the wedding (see page 71) so arrange a convenient day and time with your priest. The ceremony is similar to that in the Church of England. It begins with a welcome, an introduction and readings from the bible. After the address by the priest the bride and groom exchange vows. This is followed by the blessing of rings and the nuptial blessing. The signing of the register follows the final prayers and hymn. The couple then leave the church together. (If the marriage is taking place within a mass, the mass continues after the nuptial blessing.)

Jewish

At the ceremony the groom arrives with his father and best man and sits in a pew at the front of the synagogue. When the bride arrives the groom moves under the *chuppah*. The bride is then escorted by her mother and/or future mother-in-law (or other female relatives). When the bridal party reaches the *chuppah* the bride stands on the groom's right underneath it, with the bridesmaids behind. The rest of the party stand on either side. The ceremony starts with psalms, and the rabbi chants benedictions at the beginning and the end. After the groom has made the statement 'Behold you are wedded to me with this ring according to the Law of Moses and Israel' he places the ring on the bride's finger. A *Ketubah* (Jewish marriage document) is then read out. After the rabbi has blessed the couple a glass is placed at the groom's feet and he crushes it. Finally the couple sign the register (unless they have already had a civil ceremony).

Nonconformist or free church

All Christian marriages, with the exception of the Orthodox Church and Quakers, are very similar to the Church of England and as far as the marriage vows are concerned they are virtually identical (see pages 71–72).

Quaker

The occasion is almost without ceremony, taking place during a Meeting for Worship. At the start an explanation of the procedure is given. The couple then stand up and exchange vows. After they have done this they sign the Quaker marriage certificate with two witnesses. The certificate is then read aloud by the registering officer. Friends can then bless the couple and offer their support. At the end of the meeting the couple and the registering officer sign the civil register; those who wish can sign the Quaker marriage certificate.

Insurance

14

Because you are probably spending a large amount of money and putting a lot of time into planning your big day you may consider arranging insurance. However, before taking out a policy and make sure that you really need it.

Choosing the right policy

Any insurance broker should be able to recommend an appropriate policy to cover your wedding. On average, comprehensive insurance cover should cost about £50. Make sure you read the small print.

The main reasons why you should consider having wedding insurance are:

- to cover you in the event of tragic circumstances (if either of you or a close relative dies and the wedding has to be cancelled as a result – check who the insurance company means by 'close relative'
- in the event of one of your suppliers going out of business before your wedding.

You may find that a wedding insurance policy duplicates insurance that you hold already. Usually an 'all risks' house contents insurance policy will cover most things. Wedding insurance will only cover your wedding dress for a few days, whereas your contents policy will cover it long-term as long as you let the company know.

If one or more of your suppliers lets you down on the day – for example, your florist does not turn up – you are more likely to sue the supplier (see page 79) than claim on your wedding insurance. Check that each supplier has its own insurance.

Most people have some form of life insurance. So if a close member of the family dies, the wedding insurance will again duplicate the life insurance; you cannot claim on two policies.

If a guest suffers an injury at your reception he/she is more likely to sue the marquee provider or owner of the hotel than the bride and groom. If the accident results from negligence on the part of the couple or their relatives, house contents insurance should cover it.

House contents insurance will also normally cover legal fees, and the limits are usually higher than those offered with wedding insurance.

Insurance checklist

- If you are having your reception at home you must inform your house contents insurance company because if anything goes missing during the reception your policy might be invalidated owing to the fact that you have had lots of people visiting your house. Informing the company in advance that you are having a reception at home will also help in the event of a guest suing you for injury to him/herself at the reception.
- Also warn your insurance company that you are due to receive a large number of presents. In the event of theft the company will know not to expect receipts; confirmation of what was bought from the

wedding list can come from the department store and is usually accepted by the insurance company.
- Check with your insurance company that your gifts are covered if they are on display at the reception.
- If you are considering cancelling the wedding, first check with the insurance company that it is going to pay up and how much money you can expect to receive. Check the excess and limits of claim.
- Make sure the insurance company is part of the insurance ombudsman scheme. Brokers are regulated by law but anyone can set themselves up as an insurance provider.
- If you are going abroad for your honeymoon and will be participating in dangerous sports, (scuba-diving or white-water rafting, for example) make sure that the policy covers them.
- If you are getting married abroad check that your travel insurance covers your dress, any gifts that are taken abroad, expensive jewellery (again, this could be put on an 'all risks' house contents insurance policy). Tell your insurance company that you are getting married abroad and what you are taking with you.

When things go wrong

When you prepare for a wedding you enter into various contracts, for example, for the wedding dress, car hire, flowers, reception, caterers, photographers, gifts, holiday etc. The Sale of Goods Act 1979 (as amended) states that goods bought from a business must comply with their 'description and be of satisfactory quality', for example, if you ordered red roses from a florist you should not receive pink carnations, and a gift of a spin dryer should spin. The Supply of Goods and Services Act 1982 (common law in Scotland) states that 'services' supplied by a business should be carried out with 'reasonable care and skill', for example, hired cars should not break down, marquees should not collapse and photographs should not be blurred. Where travel and accomodation for the honeymoon is booked through a tour operator, the Package Travel Regulations 1992 give added protection in the event of a sub-standard trip or the tour operator going bust. Remember, different people in the wedding party will have different contracts with the various service suppliers, for example, an aunt might have paid for an inedible wedding cake, a cousin might have bought a defective toaster, while the bride's father paid for the reception and the couple paid for the honeymoon and the photographs – it is up to each of these parties to pursue their respective claims.

If something goes wrong and cannot be rectified before the wedding, you may be able to claim for financial losses and loss of enjoyment suffered. Where contractors know they are providing services for a wedding, the loss of enjoyment factor is likely to be greater than usual, for example, the ill-fitting dress, over-exposed photographs or ruined honeymoon will be more significant due to the one-off nature of the event. Your complaint should be made courteously and clearly to someone in management, followed up in writing (keep a copy), and pursued with polite determination. If the contractor does not compensate you satisfactorily, your best option will probably be to make an application for compensation to your local small claims court (sherrifs court in Scotland).

Appendix
Wedding Law

Anyone getting married in the UK must meet the legal requirements, whether they are having a civil wedding or a religious wedding of any denomination.

The law in England and Wales

The basic rules that apply to all marriages in England and Wales are:

- the couple must be of different sexes
- you must be aged 16 or over but you need your parents' written consent if you are under the age of 18
- you must be free to marry
- you must have two witnesses
- the wedding must take place in a district register office, in any premises approved by the local authority for marriages (hotel, stately home etc.), in a church or chapel of the Church of England or Church in Wales, in a military chapel, a synagogue or in any other place of worship that has been registered by the Registrar General for the solemnisation of marriages.

The service may not be conducted privately – which means that the doors may not be locked during the ceremony, thereby preventing entry of uninvited observers – or outside. The marriage (both civil and religious) may take place on any day at any time between 8am and 6pm and need only be in front of two witnesses, who can be total strangers to each other and to you. (These restrictions do not apply to Jewish or Quaker weddings.)

The law in Scotland

Marriage law in Scotland differs in a few crucial ways. The minimum legal age is 16 whether you have parental consent or not.

There are no restrictions on the time or place at which a religious marriage can take place as long as the legal and civil requirements are met. In theory, you are free to marry outdoors at midnight if you can find a minister to conduct the ceremony. If you want to get married on a boat it must be tethered, and if you are marrying in a hot-air balloon it must be anchored to the ground. However, civil weddings in Scotland must take place in a register office so the ceremony has to take place during office hours.

Documents required for marriage

For a civil wedding in the UK, when making a marriage application to the registrar you should take your birth certificate or passport. For a church wedding you will need to show your certificate of baptism to the minister (and confirmation certificate, in the case of the Roman Catholic Church). Most churches require at least one of you to be baptised. If you are marrying for the second time you will need to show your decree absolute or the death certificate of your former spouse. If you are under the age of 18 consent from your parents or guardians will normally be required.

Setting the date

Until very recently once you gave notice of your intention to marry to a registrar you would be issued with a certificate valid for only three months. But now, in the case of both civil and religious weddings in England or Wales, the date of the marriage can be set for up to a year in advance. In Scotland, however, setting the date has always been left to the discretion of the minister or registrar, providing the date meets with Scottish legal requirements.

Church of England weddings

If you are getting married in an Anglican church you should discuss with the minister whether you are going to have the traditional service (*Book of Common Prayer*) or a modern form of service (*the Alternative Service Book*). You should agree the form of service with the minister.

Marriage by banns

If either (or both) of you lives in the parish where you are to marry, the minister will arrange to have banns read in the church for three Sundays prior to the wedding. (These are usually consecutive Sundays.) It is usual for the couple to be present on at least one Sunday. After the third reading you are issued with a banns certificate. Without this certificate you cannot get married. A fee of about £17 is charged for the reading of the banns and the certificate. The purpose of the banns is to make public your intention to marry and to invite any objections to the ceremony taking place. If one of you lives in another parish, the banns must also be read in that church and a second certificate obtained. You should agree the date of your wedding with the minister at the earliest opportunity. The banns will be read close to the date of the wedding.

Marriage by common licence

This is used where either (or both) of you is a national of a country outside the old Commonwealth, the European Community and the United States, or where there is insufficient time to call the banns. As with banns, one of you must be living in the parish where you are to marry, and the minister will be able to advise about applying for the licence. Where a licence has been obtained no banns are called, but an affidavit – verifying the details given and that there is nothing in law to prevent the marriage – has to be sworn. You should note that common licences are not available if one of you has been divorced (and the former spouse is still living) and it is also a requirement that at least one of you must be baptised. The fee for a common licence is currently £53.

Marriage by special licence

This licence is issued on the authority of the Archbishop of Canterbury, and exceptional reasons why one of the other preliminaries above cannot be used must be given. It is generally used where neither of you is resident in the parish where you wish to marry or if the wedding is to take place in an unlicensed building, such as a private chapel. These licences are issued by the Faculty Office, which you should approach after consultation with the minister. Again, special licences are not available where one party is divorced, with a former spouse still living, or where neither party is baptised. The fee is currently £120.

CIVIL WEDDINGS IN ENGLAND AND WALES

A civil wedding is one that takes place in a register office or other building approved for civil marriage.

Unless you are marrying in the Church of England or Church in Wales by banns or by common licence or special licence you or your partner must give notice to the superintendent registrar at the register office(s) for the district(s) where you live (not necessarily the register office where you are going to get married). This notice can by given either by certificate or by licence (see below).

You can give notice of your intention to marry a year in advance of the wedding day (some register offices accept provisional bookings years ahead) and can marry in any register office in England and Wales as long as you live in either country.

Marriage by certificate

Both of you must have lived in a registration district in England and Wales for at least seven days immediately before giving notice at the register office (if you live in the same district you need only give notice once but if you live in different ones you must give notice in each).

When the superintendent registrar has accepted the notice, it is then entered into the marriage notice book and also displayed on a public notice board for 21 days. This provides the opportunity for anyone who has an objection to your proposed marriage to make a statement.

The fee for giving notice is £21 and this will have to be paid twice if you each live in separate districts. You will also have to pay a fee of £30 to the registrar for attending your marriage at a register office. After the 21 days you will be issued with a certificate of marriage. This is not the same thing as a marriage certificate, which you can request after your wedding, but a document that is held at the register office until the day of your wedding. If your notice of marriage is being displayed in two districts you must still collect both certificates of marriage prior to the wedding as you will be asked to produce them before the ceremony can go ahead.

The date of your marriage can then be set to take place at any time within a year of the date when notice was given. If you find that you wish to postpone the wedding beyond that time you will have to apply and pay for a notice (or notices) again.

Marriage by licence

If you cannot or do not want to wait for the 21 clear days to pass before marrying, you should apply for a superintendent registrar's certificate. If either one of you (it need not be both) has been a resident in a registration area for 15 days prior to giving notice and all your documentation is in order, a licence can be issued (the other party must be in England or Wales on the day notice is given). This means the marriage can take place after one clear working day following the day on which you gave notice of your intention to marry.

The notice of a marriage by certificate and licence is not posted publicly. There is an extra charge for the licence which means the marriage would cost £97.50.

MARRIAGE IN SCOTLAND

For both civil and religious weddings in Scotland a minimum period of 15 days' notice must be given to the office of the superintendent registrar before the proposed date of marriage, although four to six weeks' notice is preferred. Banns are no longer required for a religious ceremony. A schedule is then issued to the applicant seven days before the religious ceremony. It must be given to the minister before the service. For a civil wedding the schedule remains at the register office.

The order and content of the marriage service may be amended, and the minister may agree to the inclusion of non-scriptural readings of poems or prose. Prior residency in the parish or district is no longer required.

MARRIAGE IN NORTHERN IRELAND

To be permitted to marry in a church, one of you must have been resident in a parish/district for seven days before giving notice of your intention to marry. To marry in a register office, one of you must have lived in a district for at least 15 days and the other for at least seven days.

ROMAN CATHOLIC WEDDINGS

Anyone having a Roman Catholic wedding must give notice to the superintendent registrar (see pages 83–84), and in some cases the registrar must be present at the religious ceremony. Unlike Church of England or Church in Wales and Scottish ministers, Roman Catholic priests are not allowed to act on behalf of the state.

A Roman Catholic priest may insist on a lengthy period (usually at least six months) of notice of your intention to marry as it is regarded as essential for you to prepare properly for such a serious commitment. If the marriage is mixed (i.e. one of you is not Roman Catholic), the parish priest will have to apply for special permission on your behalf. Both ministers can attend the ceremony. Banns are required to be published in both of your parish churches.

Jewish weddings

Jewish weddings can take place anywhere – in a synagogue, private house, hired hall or in the open air – as long as they are held under the *Chuppah* or wedding canopy, which symbolises home, and the couple has the necessary legal documents (marriage licence or certificate for marriage, see pages 83–84). The ceremony can be celebrated at any time, except during the Jewish Sabbath (from sunset on Friday until sunset on Saturday) or on festival or fast days. It must also be performed in the presence of 10 men, and two witnesses who are not related to either bride or groom. Both the latter must be of the Jewish faith and free to marry. If either the bride or the groom is not Jewish, he or she must convert before getting married. The process is long and demanding, involving instruction and an examination. The Jewish wedding ceremony is recognised officially by the State. You can, however, if you wish, have a civil wedding and then have a religious ceremony at another time. Most couples, where both partners are Jewish, opt for a Jewish ceremony under Jewish auspices. The groom must be a member of the synagogue in which the couple is to marry.

Nonconformist or Free Church weddings

Nonconformist or Free Churches such as the Methodists, United Reformed Church, Baptists and Presbyterians and the Society of Friends (Quakers) and the Orthodox Church all require you to go to your local register office and apply to the superintendent registrar for either a licence or certificate (depending on the time you have available before you intend to marry). Whether you will need a registrar to attend the religious ceremony itself depends on whether there is a person in your place of worship licensed to act as a registrar (usually this is the minister) to witness your marriage. In addition to the 'authorised person' the marriage must be witnessed by at least two people who are at least 18 years old.

QUAKER WEDDINGS

The Society of Friends has its own registering officer, who is allowed by law to witness the marriage and signing of the marriage certificate. Quakers wishing to get married must apply to the registering officer of the monthly meeting of the area in which they intend to get married. Ideally, they should do this at least three months before the planned date (and certainly no fewer than six weeks before). The couple must then complete a declaration of intention of marriage. All the legal requirements for a wedding in England and Wales or in Scotland must also be met. Notice of the intention to marry is then made public at the meetings.

If only one partner is a member of the Society of Friends the marriage is still usually permitted providing two letters of recommendation can be produced from adult members of the society confirming their approval of the marriage.

MARRIAGE CERTIFICATES

On the day of your wedding at a register office you can purchase a marriage certificate for £3.50. This is optional but a very useful document to have in your possession. You will both be asked to disclose your addresses at the time of your marriage and your ranks or professions. The certificate also includes your fathers' names as well as their ranks or occupations. If for any reason either of you does not wish to reveal this information there is no legal obligation to do so.

DIVORCE AND RE-MARRIAGE

Whether you are allowed, as a divorcé, to re-marry depends on the type of ceremony you wish to have.

Church of England

According to the regulations of the Convocations of Canterbury and York, 'the Church of England should not allow the use of the marriage service in the case of anyone who has a former partner still living'.

These regulations do not carry the weight of law but the majority of ministers object to divorced people marrying in church on moral grounds, even if the divorced partner is the innocent party. It is still worth discussing your hopes of marrying in church with your minister as in certain cases a service of blessing might be appropriate. Make it clear beforehand if you hope to have hymns, bridesmaids, flowers and wear traditional wedding clothes to your service of blessing as some ministers do not approve of this.

Civil weddings

You will need to provide proof of how the previous marriage ended. This could be a divorce absolute document, with the original court seal, or a death certificate or a certified copy; photocopies of these documents are *not* acceptable. In Scotland there is no equivalent to the decree nisi so you can remarry directly after the divorce is announced.

After taking personal details, the registrar will ask you to sign a declaration that you are eligible to marry. A false declaration could invalidate the marriage and may render you liable to prosecution under the Perjury Act, with the further possible offence of bigamy being taken into account.

Roman Catholic Church

If either the bride or groom is divorced the couple are not permitted to have a Roman Catholic wedding; only those whose former partner is deceased or whose marriage was annulled can have a Roman Catholic ceremony.

Jewish faith

If either the bride or groom or both is divorced they must produce the decree absolute and the Jewish bill of divorce.

Quakers

Whether or not divorcés can re-marry is left to the discretion of the Friends of the monthly meetings. The general consensus is that re-marriage following divorce should be permitted.

MARRYING ABROAD

Couples choose to marry abroad for many different reasons. For example, you might each already have children and it would be a good way of combining a special event with a holiday for everyone.

There are many travel agents who can organise both low-key and lavish weddings anywhere in the world. However, do not leave anything to chance; be sure to check all legal requirements for the wedding as they can differ from country to country. When looking through the brochure or making an initial enquiry check whether you need:

- a 10-year passport
- a visa
- your birth certificate
- return tickets to the UK
- your original decree absolute
- your original marriage certificate or former partner's death certificate
- parental consent if you are under 18 (21 in some countries)
- legal proof if your name has been changed by deed poll
- proof of vaccinations, if required.

If you require documents you should take with you either originals or copies certified by a notary, although some countries require you to send them in advance.

If your wedding is not being arranged through a travel agent check the minimum length of time you have to be resident as this can vary from two days to several months. Prior to leaving the UK find out from the consulate, embassy or high commission of the country in which you wish to marry what the legal requirements are.

The cost of marrying abroad varies depending on where in the world you want to marry and what is provided. A basic wedding in Miami can start at £135, with an additional £440 per person per week for accommodation, whereas a wedding in Disney World in Orlando will cost £1,350 for the ceremony and a further £430 per person for a one-week stay. A luxury beach wedding in Hawaii can start at £500, with a two-week stay costing £1,200 per person.

PEOPLE YOU MAY NOT MARRY

It is forbidden in the United Kingdom for a man or a woman to marry certain blood relations. However, contrary to popular belief, first cousins are not prohibited from marrying. It is worth noting that some religions do not allow marriage between other relations.

Blood relatives

A man may not marry his: mother, sister, daughter, father's mother (paternal grandmother), mother's mother (maternal grandmother), son's daughter (granddaughter), daughter's daughter (granddaughter), father's sister (aunt), mother's sister (aunt), brother's daughter (niece), sister's daughter (niece).

A woman may not marry her: father, brother, son, father's father (paternal grandfather), mother's father (maternal grandfather), son's son (grandson), daughter's son (grandson), father's brother (uncle), mother's brother (uncle), brother's son (nephew), sister's son (nephew).

The same restrictions apply to half-blood relations and persons born out of wedlock.

Adopted relatives

If the adoption was authorised by an order of the court under the Adoption Act then the above restrictions apply. These are not removed even if another person has by a subsequent order been authorised to adopt the same person.

Step-relatives

Step-relatives aged 21 or more may marry provided that the younger member of the couple has at no time, before the age of 18, lived under the same roof as the older person. Neither must he or she have been treated as a child of the older person's family. Unless these conditions are met a man may not marry a: daughter of a former wife, former wife of his father, former wife of his father's father, former wife of his mother's father, daughter of a son of a former wife.

A woman may not marry a: son of a former husband, former husband of her mother, former husband of her father's mother, former husband of her mother's mother, son of a son of a former husband, son of a daughter of a former husband.

Relatives-in-law

The law was relaxed in 1960 to allow a man to marry his former wife's sister, aunt or niece and the former wife of his brother, uncle or nephew. Under previous legislation, these unions were prohibited unless the former spouse was deceased. The revisions in the law also apply to women.

The former spouses (in either or both cases) must be deceased if a man intends to marry: the mother of a former wife, the former wife of a son *or* if a woman intends to marry: the father of a former husband, the former husband of a daughter.

Marriage contracts

You may have read about 'marriage contracts', including pre-nuptial agreements. Despite their media popularity they are fairly rare and tend to be used only by the super-rich. The courts are not obliged to take them into consideration in divorce proceedings.

ADDRESSES

Division of Ministries (Methodist Overseas Division)
Church House, 25 Marylebone Road, London NW1 5JR
Tel: 0171-486 5502

Episcopal Church of Scotland
21 Grosvenor Crescent, Edinburgh EH12 5EE
Tel: 0131-225 6357
Fax: 0131-346 7247

Faculty Office of the Archbishop of Canterbury
1 The Sanctuary, Westminster, London SW1P 3JT
Tel: 0171-222 5381
Fax: 0171-222 7502

General Register Office (England and Wales)
Office for National Statistics
Smedley Hydro, Trafalgar Road, Birkdale, Southport PR8 2HH
Tel: (01704) 569824

General Register Office for Scotland
New Register House, Edinburgh EH1 3YT
Tel: 0131-334 0380

General Register Office (Northern Ireland)
Oxford House, Chichester Street, Belfast, County Antrim BT1 4HL
Tel: (01232) 250000

Jewish Marriage Council
23 Ravenhurst Avenue, London NW4 54EE
Tel: 0181-203 6311

Marriage Care
(formerly the Catholic Marriage Advisory Council)
1 Blythe Mews, Blythe Road, London W14 0NW
Tel: 0171-371 1341
Fax: 0171-371 4921

Office for National Statistics
PO Box 56, Southport PR8 2GL

Religious Society of Friends (Quakers)
Friends House, 173 Euston Road, London NW1 2BJ
Tel: 0171-387 3601
Fax: 0171-663 1001

United Reformed Church
United Reformed Church House, 89 Tavistock Place, London WC1H 9RT
Tel: 0171-916 2020
Fax: 0171-916 2021

INDEX

abroad, marrying 78, 89–90

banns 16, 82, 85
best man 15, 66, 67, 68, 69, 70
   responsibilities 22–3
bridal attendants 24–5
   bridesmaids 15, 24
   chief bridesmaid 15, 24–5
   matron of honour 15, 24
   page boys 15, 24
buttonholes and corsages 47

cake 16, 18, 52–3
cancellation 78
ceremony 16, 71–5
   Church of England 10, 71–2
   civil 10, 72–3
   fees 19, 55
   Jewish 10, 74
   Nonconformist or Free Church 75
   order-of-service sheets 33–4
   Quaker 10, 54, 75
   rehearsals 17, 18, 19, 71, 73
   Roman Catholic 10, 73–74
   service of blessing 30
children at the wedding 32, 69
Church of England weddings 10, 71–2, 82–3, 87
civil weddings 10, 72–3, 81, 83–4, 88
   marriage by certificate 83–4
   marriage by licence 84
common licence, marriage by 82

divorce and re-marriage 39, 81, 87–9
dress and accessories 16, 17, 18, 19, 35–9
   borrowing 37
   glasses 39
   head-dresses 39, 47
   hiring 36
   making your dress/having it made 36–7
   second-hand 38
   shoes 17, 38
   suit or day dress 35
   veils 39

engagement 8–14
   breaking off 14
   engagement period 8–9
   engagement ring 9–11, 14
   public announcements 8
   telling family and friends 8

flowers 15, 18, 44–7
   bride's bouquet 46–7, 70
   bride's head-dress 47

buttonholes and corsages 47
church flowers 45–6
florist 44–5
reception 46
wedding party 45

gifts 14, 56–8
for attendants and best man 17, 18, 19
insurance 77–8
thank-you letters 18, 58
wedding gift list 16, 56–7

hair and beauty 17, 18, 19
honeymoon 16, 17, 19, 21, 78, 79

insurance 16, 41, 43, 76–9
checklist 77–8
claims 79
existing cover 76, 77
invitations 16, 17, 18, 26–32
addressing 32
engraved 26, 31
flat printing 26
formal invitations 26–30
informal invitations 30–1
sending 17, 32
thermographic printing 26, 31
wording and layout 27–30

Jewish weddings 10, 74, 86, 88

legal requirements 80–91
abroad, marrying 89–90
church weddings 82–3
civil weddings 83–4

divorce and re-marriage 87–9
documents 81
in England and Wales 80
Jewish weddings 86
marriage certificates 87
Nonconformist or Free Church weddings 86
in Northern Ireland 85
people you may not marry 90–1
Quaker weddings 86, 87
Roman Catholic weddings 85
in Scotland 81, 84–5
setting the date 81

marriage certificates 87
marriage contracts 91
music 54–5
bells 55
church wedding 54–5
hymns 16, 34, 54
in non-church settings 55
non-religious music 55
organist and choir 16, 18
reception 68

nerves, last-minute 14
newspaper announcements 8, 14, 18
Nonconformist or Free Church weddings 75, 86
Northern Ireland 72, 85

Orthodox Church 75, 86

page boys 15, 24
passports 17, 21

INDEX

paying for the wedding 7, 11–12, 15
photographs and videos 15, 40–3
   albums 42
   costs and extras 42, 43
   insurance 41, 42–3
   package deals 41–2
   video service 42–3
pre-nuptial agreements 91

Quaker weddings 10, 54, 75, 86, 87, 89

reception 16, 18, 19, 59–70
   caterers 16, 17, 62–3
   children 69
   drinks 64–5
   entertainment 16, 68
   flowers 46
   going away 68–70
   marquees 60–1
   own catering 63–4
   receiving line 66
   seating plan 18, 19, 66–7
   toastmasters 16, 65–6, 67, 70
   toasts and speeches 67–8
   venue 15, 59–62
register offices 10, 35, 55, 83

rings 9–11, 14, 17
Roman Catholic weddings 10, 73–4, 81, 85, 88

Scotland 10, 72, 81, 84–5
second marriages 12, 35, 39, 81, 97–9
setting the date 81
special licence, marriage by 83
stag and hen nights 18
stationery 16, 18, 26–34
   invitations 16, 17, 18, 26–32
   order-of-service sheets 33–4
surname, changing 17, 18, 20–1
synagogue 45, 74, 86

timetable 15–21
transport 16, 48–51
   horse-drawn carriages 48, 49
   parking arrangements 51
   vintage and veteran cars 49–50, 51
   wedding cars 16, 48, 49–51
trousseau 17

ushers 23–4

wedding organisers 12–13
wedding shows 13

Here's just a flavour of some of the reports planned for future issues of *Which?*

- Water supplies • Holiday money • Car warranties • Contact lenses
- Internet service providers • Fridge freezers • Mortgage advice
- Cutting fuel bills • Small family cars • International phone calls
- Endowments • Sending money abroad • Buying a cooker
- Hiring a car abroad • Private medical insurance

So why not take up our trial offer today?

SUMMARY OF OFFER

3 free issues of Which? as they are published • Just fill in the delayed direct debiting instruction below and post it to Which?, FREEPOST, Hertford X, SG14 1YB • If you do not wish to continue beyond the free trial period simply write to us at the address above, and to your Bank/Building Society to cancel your direct debiting instruction, before the 1st payment is due • Your first payment will be due on the 1st of the month 3 months after the date you sign the mandate (so for example, if you sign the mandate on 15th August, your 1st payment is due on 1st November) • No action is necessary if you wish to continue after the free trial. We will send you Which? each month for the current price of £14.75 a quarter, until you cancel or until we advise you of a change in price • We would give you at least 6 weeks notice in advance of any change in price, so you would have plenty of time to decide whether to continue – you are of course free to cancel at any time.

Offer subject to acceptance. Which? Ltd, Reg in England Reg No 677665. Reg Office 2 Marylebone Road, London NW1 4DF. Reg under the Data Protection Act. As result of responding to this offer, your name and address might be added to a mailing list. This could be used by ourselves (Which? Ltd, or our parent company Consumers' Association) or other companies for sending you offers in the future. If you prefer not to receive such offers, please write to Dept DNP3 at the above Hertford address or tick the box on the coupon if you only want to stop offers from other companies. You will not be sent any future offers for 5 years, in compliance with the British Code of Advertising and Sales Promotion.

— — — — — — — — ▼ DETACH HERE ▼ — — — — — — — —

Your name and address in BLOCK CAPITALS PLEASE

Name (Mr/Mrs/Miss/Ms)	Address
	Postcode

To: Which?, FREEPOST, Hertford X, SG14 1YB

Please send me the next 3 months' issues of Which? magazine as they appear. I understand that I am under no obligation – if I do not wish to continue after the 3 months' free trial, I can cancel my order before my first payment is due on the 1st of the month 3 months after the date I sign the mandate. But if I decide to continue I need do nothing – my subscription will bring me monthly Which? for the current price of £14.75 a quarter.

Direct Debiting Instruction Please pay Which? Ltd Direct Debits from the account detailed on this Instruction subject to the safeguards assured by The Direct Debit Guarantee. I understand that this Instruction may remain with Which? and if so, details will be passed electronically to any bank or building society.

_DB9_W

Signed | Date

Bank/Building Society account in the name of | Name and address of your Bank/Building Society in BLOCK CAPITALS PLEASE

To:

*Banks/Building Societies may decline to accept Direct Debits to certain types of account other than current accounts

*Bank/Building Society Acct. No.

Bank/Building Society Sort Code

Tick here if you do not wish to receive promotional mailings from other companies ☐

Postcode

——— **NO STAMP NEEDED • SEND NO MONEY** ———